scenery

Poets Out Loud

Elisabeth Frost, series editor

scenery

a lyric

José Felipe Alvergue

FORDHAM UNIVERSITY PRESS

New York   2020

Visit us online at www.fordhampress.com.

Library of Congress Control Number: 2020909516

Printed in the United States of America
22 21 20   5 4 3 2 1
First edition

to my family

scenery

material apparatus of a theatrical stage

violent encounter between two or more persons

in front of, before (as in evident)

for a *SCENERY* imperative to empathy

CONVICT LEASING
"Hogtied," John L. Spivak (1932)

convict (n). from the verb form, convict: to convince in argument; to "over come"; to impress. From the Latin, convincere.

Between the mid 19th- and early 20th-centuries states declaring themselves too impoverished to maintain prisons and prisoners would lease out convict labor to railway and mining contractors or large plantations. The practice became especially prevalent following the Civil War.

False convictions, theft of bail money, and identity fraud supplied the lease system with so-called convicts.

The convict becomes recollection, which labor
gives over to the grammatical. A body is bent and
turned weight on the shovel, a muscle pulls an arc
an extension at the hoe, the hammer. A stance
upon the ground shaken by strike and arranged by other punish
the pull of ties and spikes utters an optical situ ments docu
ation for which discipline, as we are taught it, mented
offers itself without endangering the objectivity of include the
American liberty. rack, wherein
a convict's
arms are
pulled in front
of them
while they
stand in the
sun
"Convicts working in unison by singing," reads a until their
caption by John L. Spivak in 1932, whose descri body forms
ption of the image makes an aesthetic predicament a
out of the ethical paradox depicted by the chain ninety degree
gang. "Rhythmic movement is necessary," he angle.
continues, "to avoid injuring one another while
bending or rising." The way history sometimes
projects memory forward, erasing the breach of
the moment that is the present, makes of the scene
        a dimension interpreted objectively as the

Children often become frustrated when building on a macroscale.
Their hands, better suited for focusing on the touch and manip
ulation of individual objects, can't keep pace with the vision
of, for instance, a corral for their elephant, or a seemingly
endless highway of wooden blocks for their train. I
know that children's hands have built America. Its

naturalness of a state, *infrastructure, commerce, universities, govern*
of being in such a pose, the *ment houses, etc. The invisibility of what*
naturalness of law to keep the *transpired, which is to say not only the*
body there under watch, near *work but also the death, and also all*
death like the gray pixelated skyline. *the other fidgeting and research*
To work towards that death, to overcome *that is the physical world of a*
it, sing it, to praise a faith in it. Recollect it. *child's body, this is all a lost*
Cast it forward, in front of us, to recollect it, and *opportunity for a new*
so on, this becomes the work which convinces us of *language, for educat*
the physical grammatical legitimacy. The image turns it *ing parenthood.*
to brush and the song to syncopation. Convince before the *All unknown*
heavenly angels and the screen through which song projects *scenery.*
with blurred echoing boundaries that there is no childhood, no
age, no voice, no status with which to declare no, no recollection and
no iteration, no life which the courts precede with examples and history.

One star in the east,/ One star in the west,/ and between the two there ain't never no rest.

The lease system signals a theatricality to American abolition. The staging of rights and the commitment in performance belie the reflexive self-awareness of faith in being liberal, being a people of rights. A culture of belief.

While it leaves behind black and white photos scattered around archives [stories of possibility, of a forwardness to memory, of the uniforms overcome, of progress accommodated] the transformed land, the built carceral networks squat like stumps throughout these states. The benefit and the reward of work made invisible by classifi cation still circulates. Forced incarceration is coeval to labor without contract | but the contract is a legality, but the legal is a logic premised on crime, but crime is a
racialized grammar that we learn as we build :

Lost childhood is a ghost in every echo of public discourse.

Alabama   Arkansas   Florida   Georgia   Kentucky   Louisiana   Mississippi   Nebraska   North Carolina   South Carolina   Tennessee   Washington

there are blocks, pillars, and slabs of beams. A is building with buildingstones there are blocks, pillars, slabs and beams. B has to pass the stones, and that in the order in which A needs them. there are blocks pillars slabs beams For this purpose they use a language consisting of the words block, pillar, slab, beam. A calls them out—B brings the stone which B has learnt to pass

I was
not prepared for my son's own act of defiance to this
world. To be gray at birth. To hold his breath. To pause
upon his entry into this fortress, labrynthine and confu
sing as to whose fingers will hold you and whose will
want to squeeze you and convince the breath of its
restriction. As if he looked upon this photograph with
me and paused, holding himself by the diaphragm in
anticipation of hearing the young Black man scream out
in some human actualization of order and sense, not
wanting his own breathing to obscure the photograph's
rationale, evidence that the method of torture might not
undo the project of humanity, which, in the history of
my son's own awareness cultivating inside his mother's
body, captures everything. The anticipation was like
warfare I imagine. Though one where you are either
unarmed, holding nothing but another person or your
tied to an object you might creatively subvert, as if to say improvise with, if not for being bound to it
ownself, or where you hold a weapon you don't know
how to use. With nothing but a determination that is life itself.

The gravity of a prisoner's convictions in the Lease System could range from mere fisticuffing, hogstealing, or other misdemeanor crimes like carrying a concealed weapon—a crime, as noted by George W. Cable in 1880, common among whites though often overlooked.

My son's voice at times, pressing as it does to the limits of his body, is an investigation. How far will ribs expand. What is his. Who is it that is that his. Who is the one feeling skin stretch or the bones move. A word without contrast fills the rooms during his research. Like a cheek, or greasy finger imprinted against windows facing the street. Fills the smallest spaces between fur on cats, suprised by how voice might travel like fingers along their spines. His language is a filling that seems to not end until spontaneously consonants break the song of a voice. One that until then was the universe itself.

While some 1200 convicts during the year 1880 were leased in the system fewer than half were serving sentences of 10 years, many sentences of less than 1 or 2 years. 10 years was the maximum amount of time an over worked convict in the system was expected to live. In Tennessee, Cable uncovered 12 boys under the age of 18 leased in the system, with each serving sentences of less than 1 year. In North Carolina there were 234 convicts under the age of 20 lease d in the system.

We use words to play at some sort of vision, to build assemblies to protect ourselves from the unique injury that can be invisible, subjective. How do I teach my son the history of the will ful words that have broken skin? That are necessary to know, their genealogy in the language we build, so that he recognizes hi mself amongst others, so he may join in their injury as an engineer would who knows the keystone, which once unsettled, might bring the assembly into a new composition.

Our sound is a field sometimes. One where things are
moved by their influence on each other. With no
judgement as we know. To witness is to give it
Captu
re.   **to detain that sound in a camp of tortured stillness.**

Because I am Willful is a word often used to be kind without *Sometimes my*
discipline kindness. To be generous by capturing in a word. It is *students ask*
categorical. Do we learn about paternalism through *how I*
histories of violence? To have been violated? To be *can read*
one who studies violence is seeing influence. What is *that word*
influence by other names. Learning them. What is *outloud,*
truly another name is another language. Another *and I say I have*
place.   *to,*
                                                   that the
                                                   writer
                                                   meant for it
                                                   to be there
                                                   for us
                                                   to have
                                                   to reckon
                                                   with.

17

Vagrancy was a common charge in the Leasing System. Orphanhood, for children.

My son pushes a small plastic lawn mower so that
bubbles are coaxed from a spinning yellow sprocket.
The faster he pushes it, the more excited the bubbles
seem to float ino the light, bursting into the palms of
maple leaves forming a canopy above the scene of
us. Him pushing. Me watching.

our life blurring at the edge of becmoming an aesthetic predicament
moment

He pushes his lawn mower until his skin becomes
rosed and it seems to glow, to me*One time a student
asked if I would
feel the same
if I were
White,
and I said "but I'm
not."*
stone
beam
pillar
slab

18

I would burn every acre in America

touched by dulled glops of sweat from my child's burnt face.

I sit watching him push and feel weighed and immense and immobile in an anger that is mine. That has frothed among pages of study and that has no counterpart and clouds my ability to be neighborly.

Privilege and too much
television at a young age makes this anger a heroic
passion. The just. The burning vengeance. *Fo*
r a reason
I do not know
John L. Spi
vak, a photographer and journalist
chose to
fictionalize his document the risks he took,
ing of Southern stealin
convict camps. He ca g docum
lled it Georgia Ni ents,
gger. He had t lying to
o include an gain ac
appendix of ces
atrocity s
to acc
ount
for the
sto
ry.

The fiction moves in where the absence of real reckoning
leaves a space unaccommodated with the words
                                          we have
                                          for naming the
exertion taking place there. The commons.

Yet, the document speaks because a camera hanging around his neck was not used to bound the occasion, but rather reveal events occuring and give them, speechless from discipline, the power of conse quence. Spivak's photos stage an unstaging.

We look upon images accompanied with what we bring with us

Some images need coaxing from the archive. Some images need pause, a meditative withholding of their act, a mindful demonstration of what is present.

ON ORDER

My own memory is part of a story that projects on a screen. The lyric, I want to think, is a quill of language we sneak into the glow of this screen so that, rather than sigh with its memory, rupture the medium of its visual significance.

when memoir is the record of this ballistic act, it is also personal, it belongs to the group assembled at that moment, and changes what comes after.

There is a popular children's song I like to play for my son called "Tengo una muñeca." Traditionally, it is sung while children form a circle holding hands. As they sing they skip in one dire ction, then in the opposite direction, then back again, depending on the stanza. Children in the middle of the circle perform the lyrics of a small girl who, after taking her doll out past an appr opriate hour and the doll becomes ill, must give the doll med icine. The song ends with arithmetic:

dos y dos son cuatro
y cuatro y dos son seis
seis y dos son ocho
y ocho dieciseis

exact correlation
no study
no interpretation
memory rendered through faith in the computational

Teaching my son about regret is only possible at the moment he feels shame. And this is a tricky lesson. To feel the full shame of regret and the empowerment of learning from that shame. Being good from being bad is a privilege I'm not used to as an immigrant who grew up in a overly policed and mili tarized bordertown. Being (adj.) analytically and affectionat ely is a descriptive theory of the person I want to believe in. Being singular and symbolic. I want this possibility for my son. But I am constantly vigilant for the ballistics whistling towards us holding hands and moving in a circle within the world created by the small logic of shame, of a giving a doll imagined medicine to cure a breached trust.

We wait for the arrival of
representation to come crashing down
at the end of the song, its images
and demonstrations exhausted
from the work of display.

Recollection might be an essential demonstration in speech,
literally of voice projected into the sphere of life organized
around the consequence of recogntion, and demonstrated lessons
within a faulted system of remembered words

       time
       arrangement
       authority
       community

I don't trust the optimism
it seems I'm asked to burden
myself with at every turn

upon finding myself unheld
following the event of looking
upon the catastrophic evidence

of order

nihilism, to me, recognizes the failure of order through
the remix, riotous even, of what can be restored together from

> the past
> without
> boundary

One star in the east,/ One star in the west,/ and between the two there ain't never no rest.

"When reason realized that with the help of number it had organized all the foregoing, it called number divine and almost eternal. And so it grievously tolerated that the splendor and purity of number should be somehwat clouded by the material sound of voices. Now number is a mental construct and, as such, ever present in the mind and understood as immortal. Sound, on the other hand, is temporary and fleeting, but can be memorized. – this hybrid of senses and mind came to be called music."

there is a site called St. Augustine's Slave Market in Florida   stone   pillar   slab   beam

convict   child   market   slave   photo camp

I remember why I began
this –
to be naturalized
is one
thing
to be
born American
however
my son's body
acquired
the weight of
meaning laden
hues
before
even
opening
his
lungs
to
the light
of
our scene
–

to what extent is his race the marker
of a consciousness, adaptive with the
world that springs in a cycle—history
and repetition and discpline—when
it has yet to be forced into position

in baroque paintings in photographs in
maps people seem objectively aware
of the situation for which their own
commitment in staging is imperative

to what extent are his early examinat
ions into the ends of his autonomy the
equally imperative signal to me that my
role should be holding the bottle steady
so that he may with his smaller hands
properly light the kerosene soaked rag

There is no neutrality in the apocalypse of emotion. What we call lyric.

The riot is always new form to this arrangement, a porousness
and there is nonetheless an afterwards. The riot is   impressed by
always forward remembering, a syncopation the   the fire ant, the
photographs can't keep speed with, but nonethe   thread marks
less a speed the image provokes. A temporality   burned into
within which the possible is kept in anticipation of   wrists, redness
its own forthcoming potential as fugitivity.   allowed to
     crawl over
     defenseless skin

If the fugitive is a convict who eludes custody, avoids capture, one might argue that there is freedom. Though it is a freedom at the expense of liberty.

Life is the constant pursuit of slipping through an other's fingers. Of living against an other's touch.

The convict camp seems to me an odd inverse of the fugitive camp, of a forti fication either made or subverted for the purpose of remaining together.

As childhood is a magic in the inverse of the lesson which holds the initial experience and that which we call world.

In preparing to se
e the world through my son's
life I find myself obsesse
d with a kind of study
that is a bracing
for impact.

FORT NEGRO
ALBERY WHITMAN'S SWAMPY WOOD

The poorest black that came upon their shore,
To them was brother — their own flesh and blood, —
They fought his wretched manhood to restore, —
They sound his hidings in the swampy wood,
And brought him forth — in arms before him stood, —
The citizens of God and sovran earth, —
They shot straight forward looks with flame imbued,
Till in him manhood sprang, a noble birth,
And warrior-armed he rose to all that manhood's worth.

(AW, Canto I, XXVIII)

Within the walls of Fort Negro over 300 Choctaw, Sem
inole, and fugitive slaves fought a concept like solidarity
between British paternalism and American violence.
Violence is the intimacy of drawing near that which must
be abjected, disavowed. The cannonball is a device of
proximity moving through time in a calculable arc, and
with spontaneous results at the point of contact. Theori
zing ballistics is akin to a predication we are supposed to
have a necessary faith in because we are taught it like
learning what words come after what words.

Black Seminole resistence in Florida is a history lesson in the shifting waters of citizenship itself, of status as the power to enact consequence—consequence a transmutable affect of the body to which supremacy attends through its fetishistic desire to unlock and yet, out of a shame for enac ting its ownself, erase. Prior to Fort Negro, Fort Mose had served as a refuge and military outpost for Native and Black fugitives who could plead allegiance to Spain and gain, in this trade, power. Like many Spanish loyals the inhabitants of Fort Mose withdrew to Cuba at the turn of the 19th-cent ury. Fort Negro came into being when British forces handed over a fortification on the Apalachicola River to over 300 Native and Black refugees of American violence. The "cit izens" of god and "sovran earth" underscore the paradox of our own liberal democracy where rights are the electing love of an authority that remains immeasurable and insu bstantial, yet entwined, autochthonous even, to the natura lized logic from which the reality of our world emerges for the circular benefit of elected identity.

The remix does not substantiate one metric over the other.
Performance, rather, implodes the objective universality of any
one predicament, any one contact point of sound to the person.

research as aesthetic distortion

The person, a promise-making.

To belong humanly and simultaneously democratically
acts out the survival of injustice and failure. Then we call
on voice, on the body, on sinew to do the plastic job of
holding together what can easily be dissected. Faith is
ballistics. To me, to the Black Seminoles counting
cannonballs, optimism is a turbulent horizon, an unsteady vista

Voice enacts context even while the demonstr
ative dimension, the enacting, transcends the
objective circumstances of what context brings
into relation. Speaking for oneself, within the
predicative circumstance of enacting the scene
of America, extends an opening to a holding
environment. A generousness that is the prospe
rity myth, the convict camp, the fugitive camp,
the detainment camp, the respirator, the family.

Rather than conclude an optimism or pessimism
from the anticipatory register of disclosure, of
voice opening the public for the arrival of the
self, I am captivated by how voicing reaches and
approaches, finds new ways of speaking that
elude capture, elude detainment, export.

Despite my aesthetic obsession, I don't think there is a we who can theorize genre without also what sounds out after all the study. What resonates and is systemica lly real no matter what. The beats following the disclosure of the clearly sung cannot be archived without the speed of capture. Such a poetics would give form to the collaborative, cooperative speech from scenery as an act against the humming of continu ity. Such a poetics is elusive.

"The Rape of Florida" ends in a stoic silence, a scene of naturalization and the hero Altassa, who fights against the authoritarian state, enslavement, and seizure, going into the new west with a conviction in futurity, yet marked as convict by the circumstances of resistant indigeneity and Black Seminole fugitivity. Whitman brings this fugitivity into the fold of an unraveling epic that involves the way territory witnesses a transformation in human activity, from the violence of the "sword" to a generation arriving with "pruning hooks and plows."

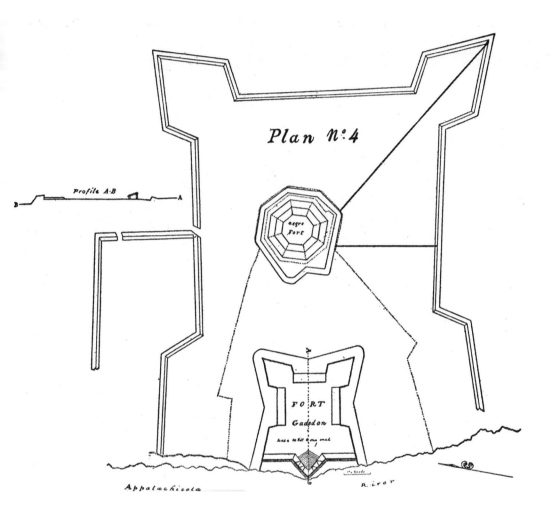

Plan Nº 4

Profile A·B

negro Fort

FORT
Gadsden

Appalachicola

River

I think about Whitman's "Rape of Florida" now in order to make sense of the deep love people feel for the same places they burn to cinder, and of the loneliness children are feeling while the metallic dandruff of quickly assembled fencing and auditorium lighting dry out their eyes and make their mouths inhospitable

   waiting for grownups who might not come back to them.

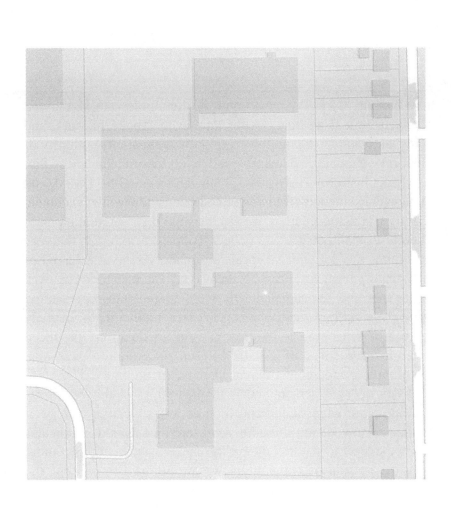

In Whitman's lyric Palmecho and the Seminoles are in the end deceived by a false treaty. After Palmecho "spoke of wars, and rights, and lands," the pirates hearing the authenticity|authority of "the brave old chief's demands" and "with inborn hate" place him in "chains instead." He, Altassa, Palmecho's daughter Ewald, and all others are shipped off to Texas, convicts, and Florida, occupied. When we talk about failure we are insisting on a colonial moment wherein to make demands has been coopted to produce the very constraints against which appeals are made. Archival research of 17th-century legal cases reveals the ways, in hemispheric contexts, indigenous and African plaintiffs were forced into representing themselves within the bounds of casta entitlements—namely degrees of separation to Whiteness—and in doing so, produced systemic procedures of disenfranchisement amongst their own communities, and against others likewise in fugitivity. The perfo rmativity of legal personhood is the becoming of this repertoire blurred at the edge of judicial archive and objective history. It implicates how we are forced to represent ourselves. It implicates how we expect to witness the performance of others before autho rity—the amount of authenticity we are allowed to employ, the proximity to authority we are permitted to endear.

I've come to know the parking lot of my son's daycare with an intimate and complicated affection for others, and as a place where my own freedom often falls short of anything righteous. I make a profound promise to a being for whom the contract is less valuable than the feathered velcro on shoes that can be tugged at when no other activity makes sense enough to engage alone. I feel his knees against my ribs for entire days. A breath of his into my neck is a net that gathers us from begining to end. There is a microscopic gene in this scene. If I were to collect it with my spit and send it through the centrifugal wonder of science I am convinced it would come back in a red enevelope. I would open it to find myself undoubte dly American. Guilty of separation. Guilty of keeping watch with my ears turned off, or maybe gruesomely tuned in to the crying and shouting, and feeling the urgency amongst my peers for the apocalyptic moment a child simply stops calling for the only thing that might keep them alive.

I teach in America. I live in America. I parent in America. I love in America. I vote in America. I read in America. I bank in America. I stare in America. I covet in America. I ujjayi in America. stone pillar block brick rock brick   brick   slab brick brick brick brick

G45 Secure Solutions

CoreCivic

GEO Group

MTC   Management and Training Corporation

Who finds this country now, exulting finds
That nature sounds the anthems of the free, —
The boundless prairie swept by restless winds,
Great forests shouting on tumultuously,
Rivers that send their greetings to the sea,
Peace-loving vales, where weed-brimmed waters run,
Broad lakes whose shade-fringed margins lisp their glee
Mountains, that prop their green heights in the sun;
And herded slop[e?]s that winter never looks upon!
(AW Canto IV, XLVI)

ALEC American Legislative Exchange Council

Serco

The Vangaurd Group

RIOT
SCOTT, WATSON, LONG

'This is a Civil War. This is not me against Mr. Watson—it's not a personal vendetta. The problems were happening before Mr. Watson and I were born.'

'He's way in front of me, his lights beaming down, going accross the streets. My heart is, like, my body's hot. And I'm nervous. And scared. Because I knew it was going to be pretty much a beating going to run from ning.'

In the opinion of the court, the legislation and histories of the times, and the language used in the Declaration of Independence, show, that neither the class of persons who had been imported as slaves, nor their descendants, whether they had become free or not, were then acknowledged as a part of the people, nor intended to be included in the general words used in that memorable instrument.

Rereading the transcript for the Phil Donahue Show in 1993, where Reginald Denny and Henry "Kiki" Watson first meet following the infamous tape of Watson holding his heel against Denny's throat while Denny lay on the ground bleeding a few feet from his truck, and with America watching on television, helicopters gathering footage from a distance, I don't think I appreciated either Watson's complicated anger or Denny's sense of history. Not in 1993 at least when I must've been around fourteen. I remember audience members being very angry. I understood Watson as a guest of the show and there being some pressure maybe in sitting up there, and I remember his shirt actually. I don't write this, thinking of Watson, Dred Scott, and another contemporary mediatized individual, Corey Long, wanting to say Watson is a hero, because that would mean the event itself was an epic plan for the culmination of itself. I don't think self-defense can be defined without one universal example of transgression, or of breached safety.

The Court established the Scott v. decision in 1859. The decision itself reaffirms settler colonial imperatives, like White annexation, and territorial dispossession, it also establishes the logic ation of racial classification as the logic towards this enterprise, and positions Black ans within an economic rendering of domain, hood and time. But it is Van Evrie's introduction that is most dangerous, and Cartwright's pseudo-biological account of ity following the decision that is most epistemologically violent.

the Declaration and the legislation and the language used in the class of persons who had been imported as slaves, nor the persons who had become free or not, were then acknowledged as a part of the people, who had become free or not, were then acknowledged in that memorable instrument.

member of the political community formed and ed to all the rights and privileges and immunities nited States in the cases specified in the Constitution. that neither they

Can a negro whose ancestors were imported into this country, and sold as slaves, become a member of the political community formed and brought into existence by the Constitution of the United States, and as such become entitled to all the rights and privileges and immunities guaranteed to the citizen? One of which rights MUST be the INTENTION AND MEANING WHEN IT WAS FORMED AND

the historic descendance of Independence or MUST the of their descendants according to its

5. WHEN THE CONSTITUTION WAS MEMBERS OF THE COMMUNITY ITS "PEOPLE OR CITIZENS." CONSEQUENTLY, THE SPECIAL RIGHTS CITIZENS DO NOT APPLY TO THEM, AND NOT BEING "CITIZENS" WITHIN THE MEANING OF THE CONSTITUTION, THEY ARE NOT ENTITLED TO SUE IN THAT CHARACTER IN A COURT OF THE UNITED STATES, AND THE CIRCUIT COURT HAS NOT JURISDICTION IN SUCH A SUIT.

WHOSE ANCESTORS WERE BROUGHT INTO THIS COUNTRY AND CONSTRUCTION OF THE UNITED NOT REGARDED IN ANY OF THESE STATES AS AND WERE NUT NUMBERED AMONG AND IMMUNITIES GUARANTEED TO

9. THE CHANGE IN PUBLIC OPINION IN RELATION TO THE AFRICAN RACE HAS TAKEN PLACE SINCE THE ADOPTION OF THE CONSTITUTION CHANGE ITS CONSTRUCTION TO CONSTRUCT AND NOW ACCORDING TO ITS ADOPTED.

violent.

There is cell phone video that compli ments the image holding of Corey Long holding a improvised flame thrower. The video is long enough to capture Richard Wilson Preston, self proclaimed Grand Wizard of the KKK, yelling "die n*****", and (after mistakenly) shooting out his gun at Mr. Long, then trying to do so with the safety on) walking away with the rest of the Unite the Right demonstrators in Charlottesville, VA. Easily melding into the white crowd, some children present, their parents, and others in bullet proof vests.

When I read to my son he trusts that I'm reading the words that form part of the object he has pulled from the shelf and walked over to me. Is it really about language? That inherent function of a kind of trust thinkers like Judith Butler theorize as the complicit site of injury? Plato the demonstration of an entertaining lie? I think of anger a lot, often. Because I usually feel it in the echo of recognizing love, and it tastes of a flavor that has failed on my tongue. Faith is a promise in the context of language as I've come to be aware of it. I wonder who, at the time of its airing, understood Kiki Watson's anger. Fully understood it. I wonder where they were at the time and I wish I would have known them, I wish I could have found the m.

THE WORD WHITE IS EVIDENTLY USED TO EXCLUDE THE AFRICAN RACE, AND THE WORD "CITIZEN" TO EXCLUDE UNNATURALIZED FOREIGNERS; THE LATTER FORMING NO PART OF THE SOVEREIGNTY, OWING IT NO ALLEGIANCE, AND THEREFORE UNDER NO OBLIGATION TO DEFEND IT. THE AFRICAN RACE, HOWEVER, BORN IN THE COUNTRY, DID OWE ALLEGIANCE TO THE GOVERNMENT, WHETHER THEY WERE SLAVES OR FREE; BUT IT IS REPUDIATED AND REJECTED FROM THE DUTIES AND OBLIGATIONS OF CITIZENSHIP IN MARKED LANGUAGE.

The image misinforms us, though there are different ways images are made and nonetheless the scene depicted was, in some manner, real. Corey Long holding an improvised flamethrower became emblematic of the counterdemonstrations in Charlottesville. They are emblematic now of our failure to have done anything whatso ever as a nation to address the Civil War occurring, the one Reginald Denny called out in 1993, the one Kiki Watson wanted to extinguish with the heel of his foot, the one he brought himself to under stand through the clouds of smoke and anger and the noise of helicopters and the burning glances of camera lenses, the one he understood at just the right moment:

I remind myself that "There is a war on *injury is mine. It* Black *belongs to me. It is generat* men." *ed when the word for it flashes as electricity in the gummy area of me, which becomes rigid and dried out from the heat of it, and full of contrast.*

The war is Van Evrie's tone when he declares . negro liberty . for the white man would render liberty impossible. The language is a broken instrument. Or it is meant to be. That is precisely the canvas I face every day with nothing but rocks in my hands.

It takes shape, what gets burned. It is a shape more
honest than the form impressed on it before it burns.
After time the impression is a city I'm told is also
my own. I'm told it is mine and of my making. I
burn it as the only way out of its cast. It becomes
unclear how much I want or don't want the inhab
itants of the city to be real. The fantasy is confusing
and is the confusion of the image that is the electric
ity which becomes part of the very gumminess I'm
told is me. At one point this gumminess was painted
according to a pinwheel of differing shades of skin
tone. Then it became a pinwheel of degrees of em
otion :

The pinwheel contains hi
eroglyphics of bodies in
different contortions I
assume are commands. I assu
me the expectation to teach
my son for the moment t
he wheel addresses him.

61

I sat in a room with my students and watched them watching Kiki Watson address them in a manner so direct and honest that the screen became the shared moment of the consequence of their being recognized, and their recognition that this man was speaking, was demonstrat ing the complexity that he had lived despite what is for some an invisible encampment.

1856
1992
2017

"Upon this act—I invoke the considerate judgment of mankind...

...and the gracious favour of Almighty God."

LYRIC

bound to the matter we subvert

Writing against conceptual poetry Calvin Bedient
argues that experimentalism, "head poetry," priori
tizes neutrality to the passion that is social. This *it seems the aesthetic*
forecloses on the poet, who, in recongizing the *war is fought over that*
shadow of elective love in the act of speech, and the *territory called the*
act of speech a corrupted legal obstacle to the meta *social*
physical scene of America itself, refuses the deter
minism of an emotional disposition celebrating *but it is*
actually the realm
always being seen and heard in the way of gratitude *we call*
to one's "place" amidst the portrayal. Of being made *personal which*
happy when the cannonballs finally reach the music *lyric, memoir,*
of resisting the terror of slowly waiting. Of being *image, up*
recognized by the heavy finger of that love. *turn in the*
ir performance

To define genre as such seems to make prom
ises about how we should see the future, or
expect from it the resolution of having learned
about ourselves, about shame or exceptional
ism.

as kneeling
fleeing
hoping
diff
erently
than
what
others
hope
and
ho
w

Theorizing nihilism comes easy to me in
the apocalypse of emotion exploding
behind my eyes when looking upon

Volver a ser de repente tan frágil como un segundo
Volver a sentir profundo como un niño frente a dios
Eso es lo que siento yo en este instante fecundo

the catastrophic evidence only. In the
moments of being convinced by it. If I
recollect only the image of my son trying to
breathe alone inside the beeping light of a
nihilistic machine, a machine without the
capacity to moralize the lifeforms it holds

Violetta Parra wrote "Volver a los 17" in 1962. I don't
know what could be heard during the invasion of Fort Negro
about 150 years prior to this song. I don't know what was
there.to hold on to, to believe in. I can imagine scenarios.
To reanimate emotion
which reason obliterates as if routine. This is the experi
ence of terror Parra responds to. It is heroic to imagine in
the remix of her voice an adolscent honesty to the capaci
ty of turning emotion into a kind of power that makes
others take notice, or regard as human voice, as if to say,
Political. Such that, even merely the mimesis of voice,
ventriloquism, is an urgency, maybe even a necessity, to
find the ear of an other. While the scenery of Ft. Gadsden
seems too overrun with tourism really to pause and listen
for what is left of such feeling. America is over run with
this same busy sound. It's the cackle of a market place.

can a poem represent us as we should be?

What's wrong with calling upon the heroism of survivng
a spontaneous journey that was an other's, The Other's,
planning? *does it require the classification of genre?*

Doesn't it become the most beautiful of strate
gies at that moment, which is to say, througho
ut its unending panorama?

O poem.

O son, a smile of
yours, electing in an
omnivorous manner,
yet...

Let it be only mine,
that reflection, its
color and infinity at
once.

o poem.

O history, are you feeling this
happen? What is the sensation
of the shifts and the electricity, the
recomposition? I imagine it cools,

not knowing the feel, the blood, in
a comforting manner just before, as
it dries. The skin wishes a more
direct demonstration to the

baroque light

to witness its election
of where my looking,
which is to say the looking,
is to
rest

SENESCENCE

on investigation

When a system has stopped
asking to be fed. This is a
death. There is a word for it,
senescence. Which is,
I think,
equal parts literal and
metaphorical. There is
a senescence to
any scenery looked upon.

In order to portray his breath as held, I have to hold it.
I hold it back. Knowing the anxiety.

Each word is a flaky assembly of
cells that will explode painfully
at the location where they fall.

The metaphor where a photo and my memory are entangled is, as a friend describes it, gnarled. A gnar ly scene of intention and violence, of rendering and erasing.

Each word is a flaky assembly of cells that will explode painfully at the location where they fall.

It did happen. But also again. Again. And again.
And though the language is warm, saturated even,
rich and nourishing, each repitition is an abrupt
shuffle towards the edge of the system I insist upon.

Each word is a flaky assembly of
cells that will explode painfully
at the location where they fall.

shuffle

The Dred Scott decision makes mention of naturalization as a model of citizenship in America. Perhaps naturaliza tion is a model because it demonstrates how a closed system is also always a theatre of physical forms a beholder gives aesthetic morality to. My sister-in-law told us, before my son's birth, that fetuses don't actually pump their own blood. The groggy thumping overheard in sonograms or through a mother's skin is often called a heartbeat.

In the opinion of the court, the legislation and histories of the times, and the language used in the Declara tion of Independence, show, that neither the class of persons who had been imported as slaves, nor their descendants, whether they had become free or not, were then acknowledged as a part of the people, nor intended to be included in the general words used in that memora ble instru ment.

But this is not literally true. The mother's heart does the work. When the child is born into breathing and blinking and unfolding fingers, their heart flaps shut. The circuit is completed. The organ keeping them alive is starved and then also birthed. It can be taken home.

How far will relationships strain
into unsaid requirements
of love,
being loved?

How wide can small imper
ceptible distances between bodies
grow, and the concentric
circles of proprioceptive self-concept
float

In the mid 16th-century Bartolomé de las Casas and Juan Ginés de Sepúlveda debated on the fate of Amerindians. Sepúlveda viewed them as unnatural, while de las Casas argued for their salvation. For their conversion. African slaves, originating from a land without God, *bárbaro*, were not available to citizenship in de las Casas's humanism. Given the ways of the market, moreover, the practice of buying slaves from coastal African nations meant to many Europeans that slavery was contractually valid even within their emerging sense of liberalism. Conver sion is the first moment naturalization would be used to hide the literalness of anti-Blackness in the confused, and entangled circuits of metaphor in the Americas.

How wide apart can we be made to float
away from each other and

towards images that more beneficially explain
personal trauma –
away from the eye contact and the touch,
from the initial repulsion of someone else's
very human breath,
before breath becomes
the recognition of the holding power
of speaking into the impossible?

Voice, travel accross the variety of human sense. Awaken its cells.

The legality and history of anti-Blackness is a gnarled site of my own identity as a Central American immigrant, a naturalized citizen of America. To render metaphor within this situation such that the outcome resembles meaning, which is otherwise unrendered in the systemic manner of acknowledging others, this is to slow starvation down until there is an asymptotic vacuum. The chaotic and excited atomic state in the holding pattern of such impossible intimacy brings with it the awaken ing of feeling each near-catastrophic utterance spoken into anar chy. Feeling while extending closer and closer towards a thresh old into true nothingness, I am elaborated in this space. Along with my shame in erasing the reality of my child and my spouse, so to is my pleasure in rendering the metaphor that aggravates the distinction of our unions.

My emotional exhaustion is an
exhaustion over the order of words. I prefer
to let them spin around.

It is all investigation.

CASTA

De negro ẽ india sale lobo
negro 1. india 2. lobo 3.

My injury begins somewhere in
the gallbladder. Travels a canal. Is
moist, viscous. It spreads. Inhales *Are you...?*
deep behind bone and presses out *Do you speak any other*
its heel into the nerve, presses as a *language*
in addition violent term would, a word to
to English? debase the rhythm of a memory,
rather than allow a gap, rather
than allow difference without
Nation

my son was born gray

my son [was gray when he was born] he looked
asleep he was calm [appeared calm]

the color of his body held me below a spot in my
chest [a spot near the reflection from the tile on the
dullness of my body] behind the ribs [between
things] an inner music constantly playing [I'd heard
over and over and there] remixed, moved me to
speak his name. and then he couldn't breathe [to
have him taken away was] a gust to the moment so
that it might move within the walls [shifting colors
made census taking unstable] the moments of his
gray finding a way to be in the atmosphere slowly
compressing to the floor, to a spot deep underneath
the tile [my chest inside of which words grasped
onto the tails of breathtakings in hope of finding a
way out] and the reflections, the mucous and I hadn't
even begun recovering my own breath from it, to
accumulate it, or give it a box like a word to keep it
strong and brilliant. so as to hand it over to my love
for her to see.

Leading up to my son's birth I became obsessed with the history of racial categorization in the Americas called *casta*. When I look upon "Hogtied," or photos of riots, of defense, of casual and banal violence, of buildings, of bodies, of skylines, I sense we still prac tice *casta* in North America even if the words we call to each other and pass along like stones and slabs have changed, especially because of the way optics play a role in equating the aesthetic scene to an obje ctive scenery.

When we dance in a circle I sense
the anticipation of crashing
to the floor
as an excitement of disorder
and the invitation to touch some
one I love deeply

Leading up to his birth I felt, at least, that my son would avoid being made the subject of America's fetishistic violence, which it reserves almost exclusively for Black children. As if the exploratory desire, which is to say colonial imperative, to discover a magic like the fountain of youth—a richness beyond matter—emanates from the power of survival unadulterated in small Black bodies. Alive despite the terrorism which has been the Black experience in White America for centuries, as if this could be possessed once life is fished free from its vessel, through the small holes left behind as evidence. The grotesque irony is that this survival is a performance on the very stage of that terror masquerading as righteousness. Or law, which is to say Liberty, and all the methods for securing it.

The colonial memory of cannibalism is its own demonstrated fetish,
its desire turned into a thing it might feel heroic about, and not guilty of.
My writing of the memory of his birth become colorful, fetishistic flashes that
hide in their glare: time, my spouse, nurses, the instruments, my obsolescence

It strikes me, literally—and in many ways, as in it forcibly hits me, ignites within me, pierces through me, etc.—that no birth scenes are ever depicted in *casta* paintings. The baroque technique of light casts an elective naming on the sociality of the body only. Even though they are, maybe especially, children's bodies and mother's bodies, there are no scenes of giving to light so to speak (from the Spanish, *dar a luz*).

The 17th-century painting "The Birth of Saint John the Baptist" by Bartolomé Murillo, for instance, is a good example of this elective light. The future St. John is held in the center by the midwife, who washes him, a luminous doughy skin radiates to the viewer, even a prophetic glance from the child's face, while Zacharious stands in the dark overlooking the procedure unworthy to touch his son. His mother, Saint Elizabeth herself, is further off in the background in a dark bed, and only her right hand laying beside her is oddly alit.

I haven't recalled into this my own partner, and I don't particularly remember what her right hand was doing. I know I was standing beside her, equally as impotent as Zacharious because I have no biological language. My anxiety stems from this absence. I can only recall discourse. Only repeatable phrases I relied on for the two days of birth. My own elective love was, during birth, a tired forelorn gaze into the bodies of people I could not do anything for beyond the attempts of language to conspire with memory to captivate something meaningful. And even in this, for my son without a social memory to speak of, I was neither lyrically or politically useful.

In 1976 Peter de Château first established a discourse for skin to skin contact, or Kangaroo Care. The potential of this is radical. While territory promises a maternal skin, a bridge of communication that is also touch, elective love, *imperium* and *dominium*, it is in actuality only dirt. At best pine needles, or absorptive sandstone. At worst, it is a sidewalk one is forced into using everyday following catastrophe. In its conceptual demonstration, this skin is the sometimes meaningless assembly of sounds we burp out as "nation." If it were capable of the mother's skin, I
wonder–

This pessimism holds me like an environment and it is all I know to feel or recognize, even having witnessed what happens when a small unbreathing baby is placed on its mother's chest like it was meant to be there. There are no hieroglyphics for this lesson. The image of their child on their skin should accompany the social death pronounced by image after image of grieving mothers holding a shirt or nothing at all. Images should have the capacity to accomodate the flexibility of breathing syncopated amongst two sets of ribcages, and that movement should be the naming process currently, and historically, reserved to the insubstantial glow of fading baroque light painted or focused on where something more spectacular is said to be happening.

Tente en el aire: Up in the air

In the system of castas this is the racializ
ation of both a metaphorical and territorial
condition. To be rootless is the phobia to
which systems are responsive *to be rootless is the
anticipation of breath restoring color to the sur
face* Up in the air is the result of a turn, a
denigration, Torno Atrás, but maybe this
negation is also the possibility of existing
after the influence has been exhausted by its
own violence. Consumed in the silent antici
pation of breathing that is survival.

Tente en el aire hijo mío, hold on there as long as you
can. Cast a hand to us.

References:

frontispiece. Pintura de Castas, "Lobo" (Zambo): "9. De negro é india sale lobo/ negro 1. india 2. lobo 3." anonymous (c. 1780).

page 6. "Child convicts at work in the fields," (c. 1903). Detroit Publishing Co.

page 9. Ludwig Wittgenstein, *Philosophical Investigations.*

page 13. "Hogtied Convict," John L. Spivak (1932). Used with permission. "Red ants crawled all over him. His body twitched spasmadically," (Spivak's description).

page 25. St. Augustine, *On Order/ De Ordine*. Trans. by Silvano Borruso (2007), p. 105.

page 33. Composition using "Child convicts work in the fields" and "Smoke rises from Midtown buildings during the 1992 LA Riots" (Ken Lubas/*Los Angeles Times*).

page 40. "Cannon Balls from Fort Gadsden State Historic Site—Sumatra, FL," Florida Photographic Collection.

page 47. Drawing by Captain J. Gadsden accompanying his report to General Jackson on the defense of the Floridas from the files of Intelligence Division, Engineer's Corps, War Department, Washington. Shows plan of the fort on the site of the so-called NEGRO FORT destroyed in 1816, as well as outline of a larger entrenchment. The NEGRO FORT and the entrenchments were constructed by Colonel Nichols of the British Army in 1814.

page 49. Google Map image of child detention center, United States of America.

page 56. "Counterdemonstrator using improvised flamethrower," Associated Press. Used with permission. Photo by Steve Helber.

pages 57–59, 83. Dred Scott decision, published by Van Evrie, Houghton, and Co. 1859.

page 57. Reginald Denny, on the Donahue Show, air date November 9, 1993.

page 57. "Race, Rage. The beating of Rodney King," CNN Transcript, originally aired April 29, 2012.

pages 60. from "Let It Fall: Los Angeles 1982–1992" (2017), John Ridley.

page 65. Thomas Ball (American, 1819–1911), Emancipation Group 1873. White Italian marble, 45 1/2 x 27 9/16 x 21 1/4 in. Chazen Museum of Art, University of Wisconsin-Madison, Gift of Dr. Warren E. Gilson, 1976.157.

page 70. Bedient, "Against Conceptualism," *Boston Review*. July 24, 2013.

page 96. "Tente en el aire," Miguel Cabrera, 1763.

José Felipe Alvergue is Associate Professor of Contemporary Literature and Transnationalism at the University of Wisconsin–Eau Claire. A graduate of both the Cal Arts Writing and Buffalo Poetics Programs, José is also the author of *gist : rift : drift : bloom* (Further Other Book Works, 2015) and *precis* (Omnidawn, 2017).

Poets Out Loud

Prize Winners

José Felipe Alvergue
scenery: a lyric

S. Brook Corfman
My Daily Actions, or The Meteorites

Julia Bouwsma
Midden

Henk Rossouw
Xamissa

Gary Keenan
Rotary Devotion

Michael D. Snediker
The New York Editions

Gregory Mahrer
A Provisional Map of the Lost Continent

Nancy K. Pearson
The Whole by Contemplation of a Single Bone

Daneen Wardrop
Cyclorama

Terrence Chiusano
On Generation & Corruption

Sara Michas-Martin
Gray Matter

Peter Streckfus
Errings

Amy Sara Carroll
Fannie + Freddie: The Sentimentality of Post–9/11 Pornography

Nicolas Hundley
The Revolver in the Hive

Julie Choffel
The Hello Delay

Michelle Naka Pierce
Continuous Frieze Bordering Red

Leslie C. Chang
Things That No Longer Delight Me

Amy Catanzano
Multiversal

Darcie Dennigan
Corinna A-Maying the Apocalypse

Karin Gottshall
Crocus

Jean Gallagher
This Minute

Lee Robinson
Hearsay

Janet Kaplan
The Glazier's Country

Robert Thomas
Door to Door

Julie Sheehan
Thaw

Jennifer Clarvoe
Invisible Tender